Chinese Strategic Culture

AF439789

Chinese Strategic Culture

Authors

Pavan Ragavendra
Subramanyam Sridharan
Balasubramanian C

KW Publishers Pvt Ltd
New Delhi

Copyright © 2022 Chennai Centre for China Studies (CCCS)

www.c3sindia.org

The Chennai Centre for China Studies (C3S), registered under the Tamil Nadu Societies Registration Act 1975 (83/2008 dated 4th April 2008), is a non-profit public policy think tank with the following objectives.

- Carry out in-depth studies of developments relating to China with priority to issues of interest to India such as
  1. Geopolitical, economic and strategic dynamics of India-China relations.
  2. China's internal dynamics.
  3. The Sino-Indian border issue.
  4. China's relations with South Asian countries.
  5. Prospects of Sino-Indian economic and trade relations.
  6. Future evolution of China's politics and its impact on India and the world.
  7. China-India-ASEAN relations.
  8. China's emerging role in SAARC.
  9. Growing importance of South India for Chinese interaction and economic investment.
  10. India-China-Southeast Asia cultural links.
- Suggest viable solutions/policy alternatives on the basis of studies to the strategic planners and decision makers in India on issues of bilateral, regional and global importance.
- Create public opinion, particularly in South India, on the implications arising out of China's emergence as a leading global power.
- Provide a forum for dialogue with China scholars in India and abroad and give space for expression of alternate opinions on China-related topics.
- Provide a sound data base for research on China with special attention to tapping information available in Chinese language material, so as to benefit scholars, media and think tanks in India as well as rest of the world.
- Address the requirements of the business community in India, particularly informing them about the nature of emerging business opportunities and problems while dealing with China.
- Liaise with think tanks specialising on China, both in India and abroad, with the objective of exchanging views.
- Organise lecture discussions and seminars on topics of current interest.
- Interact with institutions of higher learning in South India to create awareness about developments in China.
- Bring out publications relating to China—books, edited volumes, monographs and occasional papers.

ISBN   978-93-91490-66-9 Paperback

Published in India by Kalpana Shukla

KW Publishers Pvt Ltd
4676/21, First Floor, Ansari Road, Daryaganj, New Delhi 110002
Phone: +91.11.43528107
Email: kw@kwpub.in • www.kwpub.in

Contents

Reading the Tea Leaves: Chinese Strategic Thought

Chinese Strategic Culture- Exploring the Underpinnings of Chinese Policymaking

Pavan Ragavendra

Abstract

The aim of this paper is to define present-day Chinese strategic culture and explore the central elements of Chinese strategic thought under the presidency of Xi Jinping. Chinese strategic culture is found to be built on the philosophies of Confucianism and the Tianxia theory. The policies and initiatives undertaken by Xi Jinping have been studied in order to arrive at the central themes of Chinese strategic thought—the maintenance of order and stability; the consolidation and projection of power; an emphasis on Chinese leadership along with the construction of Chinese spheres of influence. The study of strategic culture can provide insights into how a country frames its policies by tracing key historical conceptions over various subjects such as alliances, war, and state behaviour. By conceptualising Chinese strategic culture, useful explanations over why the state and various other actors have taken specific actions in various circumstances can be put forth, thus rendering the study of strategic culture crucial in explaining the recent border disputes with India. The paper will conclude with implications for relations with India by exploring possible areas of cooperation and areas of persisting conflict.

Introduction

The phenomenal growth displayed by China has occupied the centre of debates in International Relations for most of the 21st century. Today, China has the ability to counter American hegemony in multiple realms including geopolitics, trade, global governance, as well as defence, and is considered to be a great power—a title earlier reserved only for the US and the erstwhile Soviet Union. Under Xi Jinping, China has further opened itself to participation in international organisations and seeks to be a leader in global governance issues. By hosting and actively participating in several global and regional summits, China has successfully established partnerships at the regional and global levels.

With the failure of positivist theories to explain state behaviour and foreign policy, scholars of international relations have begun to turn to other methods of analysis. One framework which has been effective in explaining and predicting state behaviour is that of strategic culture. The framework of strategic culture taps into the historical and philosophical influences of a country and posits that state behaviour is a result of conditioning by these influences.

Strategic culture has been defined in many ways by several scholars. Broadly, the works on strategic culture can be divided into three generations. The first generational works argued that there are three levels of input into a state's strategic culture—a macro-environmental level, a societal level, and a micro-level which consists of military institutions and civil-military relations. The second-generation viewed strategic culture as a "tool of political hegemony in the realm of strategic decision-making".[1] Finally, the third generation defines strategic culture by using "organisational culture as an intervening variable".[2] Most scholars have studied strategic culture as a method of analysis which can be used to arrive at a list or "menu"[3] of possible decisions for states to take under particular circumstances. This paper conceptualises Chinese strategic culture by arguing that the basic assumptions that are prevalent in Chinese strategic thought can be traced back to the theories of Confucianism and Tianxia.

The strategic culture of a nation is a product of the historical experiences of its constituents; these experiences are then transformed into and solidified as specific perceptions of the nation's standing in relation to the rest of the world. Today China commands a greater position in the international order due to increases in its material capabilities as well as a shift towards being more participative in various international forums. Chinese strategic culture hence reflects these changes while containing perceptions accumulated over the nation's past, thereby allowing for key insights into its aspirations to be drawn out. In other words, the study of strategic culture provides a conceptual link between a nation's past and its desired future. There has been a wide range of perspectives on the nature of Chinese strategic thought. While scholars such as Iain Alastair Johnston have argued that a Parabellum or Realpolitik tendency is prevalent in Chinese strategic culture[4], scholars on the other end of the spectrum, such as Huiyun Feng have argued that it is primarily defensive and has a peaceful predisposition[5]. The primary task of this paper is to provide an understanding of Chinese strategic culture under Xi Jinping.

The philosophy of Confucianism was developed first by the sage Confucius, who was born in 551 BC, and later by Mencius, who is referred to as the "Second Sage".[6] Confucianism has made a re-entry into Chinese politics, with Xi Jinping frequently quoting the works of Confucius in his speeches.[7] Confucianism emphasises that a ruler must govern his country through moral standards and maintained that through morality and ethics, China would play a leadership role in the world.[8]. Chinese strategic culture also shows clear evidence of influences from the Tianxia theory. As defined by Zhao Tingyang, "Tianxia has three meanings: geographical meaning referring to the whole world; a psychological meaning that the hearts of all the world's peoples are unified, like a big family; and an institutional meaning of a world government with the power to ensure universal order".[9]

By analysing the various dimensions of present-day Chinese foreign policy, this paper argues that the central elements of Chinese strategic thought are- the maintenance of order and stability; the consolidation and projection of power; and the construction of Chinese spheres of influence with an emphasis on Chinese leadership. This analysis includes an exploration of China's domestic policies as well since domestic influences and variables make important contributions towards the strategic culture of a country. The paper concludes with a section on implications for Indian foreign policy as well as areas of persisting rivalry and potential areas of cooperation.

Central Themes of Chinese Strategic Thought and Foreign Policy

China has witnessed several changes in behaviour and strategic thought under the leadership of Xi Jinping. Under Deng Xiaoping, China underwent a period of opening up and since 1979, has witnessed phenomenal economic growth which carries on to date. The primary task that Xi Jinping strives towards achieving is the realisation of the Chinese Dream. This involves effectively building socialism with Chinese characteristics in the Chinese state and the rejuvenation of the Chinese nation. He also wishes to achieve a "strong, prosperous, modern socialist China".[10] In recent years, China has further opened itself to participation in international institutions and has undertaken ambitious projects such as the Belt and Road Initiative. China is also building its own institutions such as the Asian Infrastructure Investment Bank (AIIB), fundamentally altering the liberal international order.[11] This section analyses various Chinese domestic and foreign policies, and arrives at the conclusion that the four central elements of Chinese strategic thought are the maintenance of order and stability; the consolidation and projection of power; and finally, the construction of spheres of influence with an emphasis on Chinese leadership.

The Establishment of Order

The primary element prevalent in Chinese strategic thought is the establishment of order- which in this context refers to political stability. This theme of establishing order can be observed clearly in the domestic and foreign policies undertaken by Xi Jinping. In realising the Chinese Dream of making China a modernised and advanced socialist state, political stability plays a very key role. Xi Jinping has made the preservation of social stability a responsibility of the Communist Party and the central government.[12] The domestic order of the Chinese nation-state is preserved by the Communist Party in several ways. Firstly, economic welfare is used as an instrument to preserve political stability. Great emphasis has been laid by the Party on the alleviation of wealth inequality and on the promotion of sustainable development. Some of the measures taken towards this cause are "improvements to the social welfare system, reforms to the household registration (hukou) system, reductions in income disparity, industry restructuring, and deregulation of the services sector".[13] Furthermore, the two-hand formula of Deng Xiaoping, which involves a market-based economy and uncompromising political control, is being implemented by Xi Jinping.[14] By promoting the economic welfare of its citizens, the Party aims to cut out the causes of dissent or protest, thereby solidifying its position as China's sole ruling authority.

Secondly, Xi Jinping has promoted societal unity by invoking sentiments of nationalism and patriotism. In his speech titled "The Road to Rejuvenation", Xi Jinping states "To realize the Chinese Dream, we must foster the Chinese spirit. It is the national spirit with patriotism at its core" and emphasises the need to promote "ethnic unity".[15] There is an underlying belief that cultural pluralism can lead to dissent and political instability, and hence the Party has taken measures to incorporate the various ethnic minorities into the Chinese nation-state, often by the usage of force and violence. In the governance of the provinces of Tibet and Xinjiang, the system of regional autonomy plays a key role in preserving domestic order. In this system, "under the unified leadership of the state, regional autonomy is exercised and organs of self-government are established in areas where ethnic minorities live in compact communities".[16] However, the Communist Party holds supremacy over all the regionally autonomous bodies, providing the Party with the ability to exercise repressive practices and policies aimed at assimilating the minorities into the Han culture.[17]

The Communist Party has also increased its abilities to fight terrorism in recent times. In his speech addressing the 14th group study session of the Political Bureau of the 18th CPC Central Committee, Xi Jinping has stressed on the need to involve professional forces as well as the general public in the fight against terrorism in order to ensure that "terrorists are hunted down like rats"[18]. Furthermore, Xi Jinping has stated that there is a "need to maintain social harmony and stability in order to safeguard national security" [19]. Xinjiang's then Party Chief Zhang Chunxian also stated that security measures in the region have been upgraded and that there has been a significant drop in the number of terrorist attacks since 2015.[20] Xinjiang province's anti-terror budget was also doubled in 2014.[21] These statements provide further evidence towards the argument that anti-terrorism measures are being used towards the establishment of social order, which is a central theme in the Xi Jinping regime's policies. The Chinese government has also stepped up its counter-terrorism measures abroad by cooperating with other governments and has also upgraded its cybersecurity capabilities.[22] In Xi Jinping's speech on the occasion of the 70th anniversary of the PRC's founding, the emphasis was laid on completing the task of national reunification as well as on cross-Strait relations. These statements can be contrasted with the surging nationalist sentiments in the two regions as well as China's desire to effectively unify Hong Kong and Taiwan and establish regional order. The Hong Kong national security law passed by Beijing aims at crushing any calls of autonomy for the city of Hong Kong by criminalising acts of secession, subversion, terrorism, and collusion with foreign or external forces. The law erodes the political and judicial autonomy of Hong Kong and can be seen as a firm assertion of control over Hong Kong by the CPC.

The Tiananmen Square incident of June 4, 1989, is a major black mark in the history of Chinese politics. Beginning as a peaceful protest, it soon escalated drastically and ended with the PLA entering Beijing to violently suppress the protestors. One of the key causes of the protest was the presence of inequalities and corruption.[23] The establishment of the National Supervision Commission (NSC) has been a major step taken by Xi Jinping towards combatting corruption, and thereby achieving order and smooth functioning of the government, thereby cutting down another cause of dissent which had resulted in the Tiananmen Square incident. The Party has implemented mechanisms to ensure political unity, such as "study sessions" and "democratic life meetings". These mechanisms are aimed at eradicating the "four bad work styles", which are formalism, bureaucracy, hedonism, and extravagance.[24] The NSC ranks above the judiciary and serves as an instrument that centralises Xi Jinping's authority under the veil of institutionalising the anti-corruption campaign.[25]

The Confucian government aims at developing the virtue of its citizens through teaching. However, it becomes evident that the common populace is not expected to develop higher virtues which the ruler is expected to be in possession of, such as rightness and wisdom. The citizens are expected to develop the qualities of reverence, subordination, honesty, diligence, and correctness. The Confucian view of society considers social groups as its unit of analysis, and treats common people as an "amorphous, indeterminate mass".[26] Thus, the qualities that the common people are expected to develop are not those of virtue, but of those related to political order. Furthermore, Confucianism advocates using welfare policies towards achieving the qualities of orderliness in the citizens. In expecting the common populace to develop qualities related to obedience and orderliness, the strategic theme of establishing order becomes evident in Confucian philosophy.

The philosophy of Tianxia also advocates for the establishment of political order at the domestic as well as international levels. According to the theory of Tianxia, the ruler must win the hearts of the people, and this is paramount for the establishment of the "perfect empire". Emphasis is laid on the establishment of a good society of peaceful order, where all political levels are essentially homogenous.[27] This call for homogeneity is indeed in conflict with China's social reality, for China is home to several ethnic minorities, such as the Uighurs, the Tibetan Buddhists, and the Mongols. In order to maintain political order, regions with concentrated populations of ethnic minorities-such as Inner Mongolia, Tibet, and Xinjiang - are given the status of Autonomous Regions. Through this mechanism, the centre is able to maintain order despite the heterogeneity of the Chinese nation-state, thus meeting the Tianxia as well as the Confucian philosophy's call for the domestic order. At the international level, Tianxia advocates for a voluntary tributary system, where individual states or sub-states, which are of lesser importance, accept the superiority of the central state, and adhere to the norms and institutions established by the empire.

The Consolidation and Projection of Power

The establishment of the NSC can be observed parallel to the second theme of Chinese strategic thought under the Xi Jinping regime- the consolidation and projection of power. Xi Jinping has effectively consolidated and centralised political power by taking various measures. Firstly, Xi Jinping gains the ability to enforce ideological control by building loyalty towards the Party and eliminating his political opponents. There is a clear departure from the policies implemented by Deng Xiaoping, which involve a normative framework of collective leadership. The stature of the Central Military Commission (CMC) has been lifted to the highest civil-military authority. As the chairman of the CMC, Xi Jinping now holds complete control over the PLA and directly commands military services and operations. Furthermore, the enshrinement of "Xi Jinping thought" into the Chinese constitution acts towards the centralisation and consolidation of power in the current regime.[28] The restriction of criticism of the Party is another key measure taken by Xi Jinping towards this cause, as well as towards the establishment of political stability and order. An example of this is the infamous "709" crackdown, where 300 rights lawyers, legal assistants and activists were rounded up and interrogated by the Chinese police in 2015.[29]

The consolidation of military power is also one of the key elements found in Xi Jinping's policies. Xi Jinping has emphasised on the need to "Build up our national defence and armed forces" in his speech to the CMC as well as the need to "Build people's armed forces that follow the Party's commands, are able to win and have fine conduct".[30] Once considered a "junkyard army", the PLA has undergone a complete and remarkable transformation since the 1990s. China's announced military budget in 2013 was US$ 119.5 billion, though it is believed that certain expenditures have been excluded from this budget.[31] This clearly shows that since the beginning of the Xi Jinping regime, there has been an increased emphasis on the development and strengthening of the Chinese military. China has also invested in building anti-access/area denial capabilities in the South China Sea in case of any foreign military intervention in the region.

The projection of China's power can be observed in various domains. Firstly, there has been a marked shift in the nature of China's military actions in the South China Sea; where China has taken up more aggressive policies post-2011. Prior to the period 2009-2010, Chinese policies in the South China Sea have been largely defensive and reactionary in nature. With a more advanced and modernised fleet, China's ability to project power in this region has increased exponentially. Five incidents in the South China Sea region highlight China's aggressive behaviour- the cutting of the cables of Vietnamese seismic survey vessels in 2011-2012, the 2012 naval standoff between the Philippines and China in the region around the Scarborough Shoal, the blocking of supplies to Filipino troops stationed at the Second Thomas Shoal, the standoff between China and Vietnam in the region around the Paracel Islands, and the land reclamation and construction and militarisation of outposts in the South China Sea. Out of these incidents, the construction of artificial islands and the subsequent militarisation of these islands is the most significant, since this has given China an unprecedented ability to project its naval power from the middle of the disputed region.[32]

Secondly, with its large economy, China has gained the ability to effectively project its economic power. The usage of economic power to further political means has always been a significant feature of Chinese strategic thought. Today, China is deeply enmeshed within the global order and is a major trade partner of several countries. After its 'turn to multilateralism' in the 1990s, China has become an active participant in several international and regional institutions. Being one of the largest regional economies, China has the ability to create interdependent relations with several countries. Through this interdependency, China gains the ability to leverage towards achieving its political goals by making economic concessions, or in certain cases by threatening the imposition of sanctions. A clear example of this is the above-mentioned Scarborough Shoal incident that took place in 2012 between China and the Philippines. Vessels from both sides had engaged in a standoff over the presence of Chinese fishing boats in the disputed region. China reasserted its claim over the region and imposed informal trade sanctions on the Philippines, following which the Filipino government was forced to withdraw its stance. After the withdrawal of Filipino vessels from the region, China resumed its trade with the Philippines, and trade between the two countries increased to a greater level than before. It is evident that in this case, China has used its ability to project its economic power to effectively secure its political goals. A major obstacle that stands in the way of China's power projection is the formation of regional China-opposing alliances. ASEAN countries have increasingly sought mutual cooperation and ties with major powers in order to balance China's regional power projection capabilities. By involving countries such as the USA in the geopolitical struggle, state actors such as Malaysia, the Philippines, and India have balanced the Chinese threat.[33] However, China can still prevent these partnerships from solidifying into military alliances by projecting its economic power as a major trading partner.

Confucian philosophy also accepts the rule of hegemons, but not that of tyrants who wage war for unjustifiable purposes. The centralisation and consolidation of power under the rule of the hegemon is thus another theme that is prevalent in Confucian philosophy. Moreover, since the ruler derives his authority not from the consent of the people, but from his ability to effectively establish political order[34], the centralisation of power is justified in Confucianism.

Chinese Leadership and the Construction of Spheres of Influence

The third theme that is prevalent in Chinese foreign policy is an emphasis on Chinese leadership. After successfully becoming a part of the international order and creating webs of interdependency, China has taken up several initiatives and taken up the leadership role. By creating new multilateral institutions such as the BRICS New Development Bank, the Chiang Mai Initiative Multilateralisation Agreement, the Regional Comprehensive Economic Partnership, the expansion of the Shanghai Cooperation Organisation, and most importantly, the Asian Infrastructure Investment Bank, China has created a new role for itself in the emerging global order- the role of a leader. Xi Jinping has successfully capitalised on the withdrawal of the USA's support to the liberal international order by pushing China into the leadership position; he has also created institutions that have the ability to make up for the shortcomings of the mainstream liberal institutions such as the IMF and the World Bank. The AIIB has witnessed significant success, and also deepens China's interconnectedness with other countries. It also signals the emergence of a new "China model of development"[35] and a new Chinese global order.

Another domain where Chinese leadership is prevalent is Conference Diplomacy. China hosts hundreds of meetings of international organisations and bilateral talks every year. Through these diplomatic engagements, China gains the ability to forge ties and enhance cooperation more effectively. An important facet of the Chinese leadership is China's opposition to American hegemony. Through programs such as the Belt and Road Initiative (BRI), China has pushed countries towards accepting the emerging Chinese model as well as the centrality and importance of China. Furthermore, this effectively counters American domination.[36] The opposition to American policies is also evident in the ongoing China-USA trade war. The Chinese government has stated that the USA is following "unilateral and protectionist measures", and is wielding tariffs as a "big stick", thereby causing "disruption to the global economic and trade landscape".[37] China has also taken up a similar role in the issue of climate change. China's special envoy to the United Nations Climate Change Conference quoted that "China is capable of taking a leadership role in combating global climate change"; China has also urged the United States to remain in the Paris Accord[38]. While the fear that China may be urged to cut down on its greenhouse gases still looms large on Chinese officials, the government has sought to take up leadership for climate governance, especially in the regional context.

The recent aggressions by PLA troops on the Indo-China border highlight a departure from the previous trend of attempting to resolve border disputes with India through diplomatic channels and avoiding direct confrontations or conflicts. Furthermore, the frequency of violations along the Line of Actual Control (LAC) by PLA troops has increased since 2013[39] and can be compared to China's increasingly aggressive behaviour in the South China Sea since 2011. These actions by Beijing can be interpreted as signalling to India that it is not the sole hegemon in the South Asian region and an assertion of dominance over its close competitor in the region.

In the Confucian model, the hegemons' success "stems from their ability to forge and lead sturdy alliances with neighbouring states". The hegemon must also have the ability to defend their state without resorting to the use of force, which stems from his ability to threaten the use of his power.[40] From these statements, it is clear that Confucian political philosophy advocates the creation of alliances, and also emphasises the primacy of the Chinese nation-state in these alliances. China must hence be able to create alliances through which it can assert itself, and must also play the role of a leader among its allies.

China's leadership in various issues of global governance and in international institutions brings this analytical narrative to the fourth and final theme of Chinese foreign policy- the creation of Chinese spheres of influence. By organising a plethora of global and regional summits as well as bilateral conferences, China has increased its ability to reach out to policymakers and government elites from other countries. China's efforts in conference diplomacy fuels diplomatic successes. Furthermore, by sending delegations, tourists and diplomats to other countries, China has successfully been able to promote ties with several countries which were previously neglected by the Western powers and other developed countries.[41] The spheres of influence that China creates through repeated interactions with countries in the realms of defence, trade, and development are maintained by China's conference diplomacy efforts. China also has pushed forward the Belt and Road Initiative and has brought several developing countries into its fold through promises of mutual benefits and overall economic development. Several developing countries have created ties with China through these initiatives, especially those from the Middle-East, Northern Africa, and Latin America. By pursuing economic ties with regimes that were subjected to sanctions and criticism by the major powers such as Venezuela and Sudan, China has successfully been able to create spheres of influence that encompass developing countries from all parts of the world. Programs that facilitate the widespread use of Chinese companies in construction projects have been pushed forward by the Chinese government in several of these countries. China has pursued ties with controversial governments where the major powers have been less firm. In the case of countries such as Iran against whom the majority of the developed world is opposed, China has been willing to compromise its pursuit of economic ties.[42] In most of these engagements with developing countries, China pushes forth development projects which rely solely on Chinese capital, thereby creating dependency on itself. Through projects such as the One Belt One Road (OBOR), AIIB and the Silk Road Fund (SRF), the Chinese government has been able to export the huge overcapacity of Chinese infrastructure companies abroad. Moreover, China has signed trade partnerships with developing countries which provide new markets for Chinese exports to enter. Thus, these spheres of influence have provided China with a significant amount of control over developing countries, and this further strengthens its ability to project power and achieve its political ambitions. China's interest in being a major player in issues of global governance as well as in its participation in international institutions thus enable it to create, strengthen, and widen its spheres of influence.

In Confucian philosophy, the Chinese state must create spheres of influence by forging alliances with other countries, and by taking up the role of a leader, it must also exert dominance in its relations with these countries. The Tianxia philosophy also has similar strategic underpinnings. By viewing the world in terms of 'subordinate' state units and calling for the formation of an institutional word, the Tianxia theory puts forth the idea of a perfect 'empire'. In the Tianxia world order, sub-states that are independent in their governance, are institutionally loyal to the empire. There is a voluntary tributary system, consisting of a suzerain centre and sub-states.[43] China has effectively showcased similar strategic underpinnings by creating a network of dependency through its interactions with developing countries. Though the tributary states- which in this case are the developing countries- have voluntarily engaged in relations with the empire, they are subordinate in the structure of the world order. Various Latin American and African countries can be seen as 'subordinate' to China since they largely depend on Chinese resources and capital for development projects as well as other forms of aid and assistance- thus reflecting the strategic underpinnings of Tianxia.

Implications for Indian Foreign Policy

This final section provides a set of guidelines and recommendations for Indian foreign policy formulation, taking into consideration the four central tenets of Chinese strategic thought under the leadership of Xi Jinping. India is in direct contact with China through a shared border of 3488 kilometres. T. V Paul argues that the two countries seem to be locked in an enduring, yet managed rivalry.[44] While India and China engaged in military combat over the disputed territory of Aksai Chin- one of the several disputed regions along the LAC - only on one occasion in 1962, border disputes over the following decades were resolved through diplomatic negotiations, only occasionally leading to standoffs between the two armies. However, on June 15, 2020, Indian and Chinese soldiers were engaged in a violent military clash in the Galwan Valley, leading to the death of 20 Indian troops and an undisclosed number of

PLA troops. In the following days, the two sides managed to de-escalate the situation and withdrew their respective troops from the LAC. The border clash deepened tensions between the two governments as well as among the populations; a sentiment of anger was common among the Indian media, with nationalist sentiments rising. Furthermore, the Indian government made the decision to implement a ban on various Chinese-developed mobile applications. It is not clear whether the Narendra Modi government succumbed to the nationalistic fervour or chose to unilaterally take the decision to ban the apps. This, however, does show that the Indo-China rivalry cannot be limited to the military realm alone and is bound to spill-over into other areas of interaction between the two sides. Furthermore, the anti-China sentiment[45] evident in Indian social media seems to have a significant effect on Chinese companies in India, with Indian firms downplaying any existing links with their Chinese counterparts[46] as well as calls among the general public to boycott Chinese-made products. This raises the question of whether the Indo-China rivalry really is a "managed rivalry" and raises concern over positive engagement between the two sides in the coming years in non-military areas.

Despite the fact that the conception of both countries occurred at approximately the same time, China has far surpassed India in terms of economy as well as military strength. The reality of the large power gap between the two countries has been at the focus of India's policymakers and will continue to be so unless the rivalry between the two countries is effectively resolved. India's response to the imbalance of power has mostly been to seek to balance through alliances and cooperation with other major powers such as the United States. If India is to retain its strategic autonomy - which has been one of the central tenets of Indian foreign policy for decades - a new approach must be taken towards relations with China; one that must involve a clear understanding of Chinese strategic culture.

One strategy that can possibly lead to the betterment of relations with China is prioritising cooperation in specific areas such as increased trade, agreement on issues of global governance, and issues regarding energy security and supply.[47] Since China has been a more active participant in international institutions and is working towards developing the image of a responsible partner, India can seek cooperation through these institutions. India is a major stakeholder in the AIIB, which can serve as a forum for pursuing positive ties with China. It is indeed in India's immediate interest to play a major role in the emerging Chinese order. Though rivalling China in terms of the quantity of developmental aid is out of India's reach, it is possible for India to improve on the quality of its developmental aid. It has been made clear that developing countries are becoming increasingly dependent on Chinese capital through China's economic and development-related interactions with these countries. By providing developmental aid in the form of enriching the skills of these countries, India can indeed match up to China as a partner who supplies a more growth-oriented development alternative. This can effectively help India create its own spheres of influence. The improvement of ties with countries in the regions of Latin America, the Middle East and Northern Africa can also help India secure its growing energy needs.

India's foreign policymakers must ensure that India does not fall into a position of subservience in this emerging Chinese order. In the case of the BRI, the passing of the China-Pakistan Economic Corridor (CPEC) through the Pakistan-occupied Kashmir region has resulted in sentiments of disaffection and suspicion from the Indian side.[48] The BRI is indeed a key aspect of the emerging global order, and the connectivity that it offers in terms of trade is unparalleled; it is thus in India's immediate interests to avoid being left behind while also retaining its sovereignty and strategic autonomy. The Sino-Pakistan alliance has been one of the Indian foreign policy's major concerns. China has restrained India and suppressed its rise on several occasions through cooperation with Pakistan. Today, China is warier of deepening ties with Pakistan due to concerns over terrorism and religious extremism. India and China can indeed have further cooperation over combatting terrorism- an issue which China is focussing on increasingly. The 2019 Indo-China informal summit was conducted in a period of relatively high tensions between the two countries. India had abrogated Article 370, which provided special status to Jammu and Kashmir; the Chinese Ministry of Foreign Affairs criticised New Delhi for making jurisdictional moves over territory claimed by China. Furthermore, the informal summit between Pakistan and China which was conducted just 2 days before the Indo-China summit marked growing ties between the two countries, and India's insecurities regarding the Pakistan-China partnership were indeed being raised. Though these issues loomed before Narendra Modi and Xi Jinping, the informal summit reflected a willingness on the part of both countries to engage in bilateral dialogue and also set the stage for future summits between the two countries.

There is also an urgent need for India to develop its ties with the countries of the ASEAN bloc. India can indeed balance its Chinese naval presence through military cooperation with the ASEAN countries. Economic cooperation between India and the ASEAN countries can also counter China's ability to project its economic power in the region. Though the Modi government has begun engaging with these countries through diplomatic visits and summits, there is still a long way to go if these interactions are to solidify into deeper ties. India and the United States have deepened their ties in an attempt to balance China.[49] Though this balancing act can provide India short-term benefits, India must also be wary of becoming subservient to American regional interests.

The Indian government urgently needs to diversify and expand the country's human resources. The Indian Foreign Services is very small as compared to China's Ministry of Foreign Affairs. India must also step up its conference diplomacy by developing venues for regional and bilateral summits. It is not in India's long-term interests to merely resent China's role and capabilities.[50] By participating in China's newly formed institutions and taking up the role of a major stakeholder in these institutions, India can broaden its spheres of influence and enjoy more diplomatic successes.

Notes

1. Alastair I. Johnston, "Thinking About Strategic Culture", *International Security*, no. 4 (1995).

2. Alastair I. Johnston, "Thinking About Strategic Culture", *International Security*, no. 4 (1995).

3.

4. Alastair I. Johnston, *Cultural Realism: Strategic Culture and Grand Strategy in Chinese History* (Princeton, NJ: Princeton University Press, 1998).

5. Huiyun Feng, "China as a Rising Power", *Chinese Strategic Culture and Foreign Policy Decision-making: Confucianism, Leadership and War*, London: Routledge, 2009

6

7. Loubna El Amine, prologue to *Classical Confucian Political Thought: A New Interpretation* (Princeton: Princeton Univeristy Press, 2015), 1.

8. Huiyun Feng, "China's Strategic Culture and War", *Chinese Strategic Culture and Foreign Policy Decision Making: Confucianism, Leadership and War*, London: Routledge, 2009

9. Tingyang Zhao, "Rethinking Empire from a Chinese Concept 'All-Under-Heaven' (Tian-Xia)." *Social Identities* 12, no. 1 (2006)

10. Xi Jinping, "Achieving Rejuvenation Is the Dream of the Chinese People", *Governance of China*, China: Foreign Languages Press, 2018.

11. Matthew Stephen, "The AIIB and China's Relationship with the Liberal International Order: Insights from International Relations Theory", *Chinese Journal of International Politics* 12, no. 1 (2019)

12. Xi Jinping, "Safeguard National Security and Social Stability", *The Governance of China*, China: Foreign Languages Press, 2018.

13. John Garrick and Yan Bennett Chan, "Xi Jinping Thought", *China Perspectives*, 2018

14.

15. Xi Jinping, Align Our Thinking with the Guidelines of the Third Plenary Session of the 18th CPC Central Committee, *The Governance of China*, China: Foreign Languages Press, 2018.

16. White Papers of the Information Office of the State Council of the People's Republic of China, China's Ethnic Policy and Common Prosperity and Development of All Ethnic Groups (September 2009), Regional Autonomy for Ethnic Minorities in China (February 2005), National Minorities Policy and Its Practice in China (September 1999), Beijing: Foreign Languages Press, 2009

17. Amine Ertürk, "Similarities and Differences: A Comparison of China's Ethnicity Policies in Xinjiang and Tibet", IHH Humanitarian and Social Research Center, Istanbul: Mart 2016

18. Xi Jinping, "Safeguard National Security and Social Stability", *The Governance of China*, China: Foreign Languages Press, 2018.

19. Xi Jinping, "Safeguard National Security and Social Stability", *The Governance of China*, China: Foreign Languages Press, 2018.

20. Cui Jia, Xinjiang Strengthens Security against Terror, *China Daily*, March 8, 2016.

21. "Xinjiang Doubles Terror Fight Budget." Xinjiang Doubles Terror Fight Budget, *China Daily*, January 17, 2014.

22. "New Law to 'combat Terror, Protect Rights'." *China Daily*, February 29, 2016.

23. Denise Y Ho, "June 2014: Remembering Tiananmen: The View from Hong Kong: Origins: Current Events in Historical Perspective." *Origins*, Accessed July 21, 2019.

24. John Garrick and Yan Bennett Chan, "Xi Jinping Thought", *China Perspectives*, 2018

25. Amrita Jash. "Xi Jinping as the New 'Tianxia' of PRC: Implications of His Power Consolidation." Issue Brief No. 159, Centre for Land Warfare Studies, 2018.

26. Loubna El Amine, "Ruler and Ruled", *Classical Confucian Political Thought: A New Interpretation* (Princeton: Princeton Univeristy Press, 2015)

27. Tingyang Zhao, "Rethinking Empire from a Chinese Concept 'All-Under-Heaven' (Tian-Xia)." *Social Identities* 12, no. 1 (2006)

28. Amrita Jash. "Xi Jinping as the New 'Tianxia' of PRC: Implications of His Power Consolidation." Issue Brief No. 159, Centre for Land Warfare Studies, 2018.

29. John Garrick and Yan Bennett Chan, "Xi Jinping Thought", *China Perspectives*, 2018

30. Xi Jinping, "Build People's Armed Forces That Follow the Party's Commands, Are Able to Win Battles and Have Fine Conduct", *The Governance of China*, China: Foreign Languages Press, 2018

31. Michael S Chase et al, "People's Liberation Army Modernization: Mid-1990s to 2025" *China's Incomplete Military Transformation: Assessing the Weaknesses of the People's Liberation Army (PLA)* (Santa Monica, CA: RAND Corporation, 2015).

32. Richard Q Turcsanyi, *Chinese Assertiveness in the South China Sea: Power Sources, Domestic Politics, and Reactive Foreign Policy*. Cham, Switzerland: Springer, 2018

33.

34. Loubna El Amine, "Ruler and Ruled", *Classical Confucian Political Thought: A New Interpretation* (Princeton: Princeton Univeristy Press, 2015).

35. Matthew Stephen, "The AIIB and China's Relationship with the Liberal International Order: Insights from International Relations Theory", *Chinese Journal of International Politics* 12, no. 1 (2019).

36. Jabin T Jacob, "China's 'New *Tianxia*' Strategy and the Indian Response", ICS Working Paper, 2015.

37. White Paper of The State Council Information Office of The People's Republic of China, China's Position on the China-US Economic and Trade Consultations (June, 2019).

38. Coco Liu, "Beijing Seeks to Enhance 'Soft Power' with Climate U-turn." *South China Morning Post*, February 13, 2017.

39. Jeff M Smith. The Simmering Boundary: A "new normal" at the India–China border?: Part 1. Observer Research Foundation, June 13, 2020.

40. Loubna El Amine, "Rules and Regulations", *Classical Confucian Political Thought: A New Interpretation* (Princeton: Princeton University Press, 2015).

41. Jabin T Jacob, "China's 'New *Tianxia*' Strategy and the Indian Response", ICS Working Paper, 2015.

42. Robert G Sutter, "Relations with the Middle East, Africa, and Latin America", *Chinese Foreign Relations: Power and Policy since the Cold War*. Lanham, MD: Rowman and Littlefield, 2016.

43. Tingyang Zhao, "Rethinking Empire from a Chinese Concept 'All-Under-Heaven' (Tian-Xia)." *Social Identities* 12, no. 1 (2006).

44. T.V. Paul, ed. Introduction to *The China-India Rivalry in the Globalization Era.* Washington, DC: Georgetown University Press, 2018.

45. Inamdar, N. Can India afford to boycott Chinese products? BBC June 25, 2020.

46. Phartiyal, S. "Firms in India downplay Chinese links amid wave of anti-China sentiment". Reuters, July 1, 2020.

47. T.V. Paul, ed. Introduction to "*The China-India Rivalry in the Globalization Era*".Washington, DC: Georgetown University Press, 2018.

48. Jabin T. Jacob, "Chinas Belt and Road Initiative: Perspectives from India." *China & World Economy* 25, no. 5 (2017).

49. Frédéric Grare. "The Impact of the US Factor on India's Asia Policy." *Oxford Scholarship Online*, 2017

50. Jabin T Jacob, "China's 'New *Tianxia*' Strategy and the Indian Response", ICS Working Paper, 2015

Chinese Strategic Culture: The 'Chinese Characteristics' that Shape China's International Relationship

Subramanyam Sridharan

A Background

Of late, we constantly hear of 'Chinese Characteristics' being attached to any move or initiative emanating from China. For example, the latest Paramount Leader of China, Xi Jinping's "Thought on Socialism with *Chinese Characteristics* for a New Era" became quite a talking point after the 19th National Congress of the CCP in October 2017. This is, surprisingly, not the first time that this jargon has been used by China, but it certainly caught the imagination across the world after Xi Jinping (in)advertently popularised it.

The Strategy paper released by the White House on May 20, 2020,[1] "The United States' Strategic Approach to the People's Republic of China" defines the 'Chinese Characteristics' as follows: This system is rooted in Beijing's interpretation of Marxist-Leninist ideology and combines a nationalistic, single-party dictatorship; a state-directed economy; deployment of science and technology in the service of the state; and the subordination of individual rights to serve CCP ends. But these are ephemeral and shallow and do not address the more underlying factors that define these '*Characteristics*'.

As we know, China has an uninterrupted and recorded history of over 2200 years of Imperial rule by various dynasties, even more, if we consider the *Shiji* records by historian Sima Qian and his father. There was a brief period of democracy early-to-mid last century which was snuffed out by the events of the Long March leading to the eventual control of China by the Communist Party of China (CCP). Essentially, this means that the Chinese have had an uninterrupted autocratic rule or central authority for nearly twenty-five centuries.

As is true of such things in ancient China, the term 'Chinese Characteristics' is in itself not new, The Tang-dynasty Empress Wu Zetian (8th century CE) had to impart 'Chinese Characteristics' to Buddhism because the Chinese Emperors and the Empress could not be seen bowing to a high Lama. The Empress even gave a female form to the Buddha! It piques our interest therefore to understand exactly what is meant by this phraseology.

Therefore, from the Wu Zetian example, one might be tempted to interpret 'Chinese Characteristics' as anything which is decided by the authority and enforced, but it is far more complex than that. For example, the Beijing branch of the Japanese clothing chain Uniqlo became infamous in 2015 after an obscene clip of a couple in the shop went viral. The Chinese Cyberspace Administration said that the clip "severely violated socialist core values of China".

Therefore, this is a civilisational aspect and like in understanding any ancient civilisation, there is a lurking danger of either profound generalisation or oversimplification. In the realm of 'Chinese Characteristics', there is little or no scope within China for debates or opinion-making or such democratic practices. People are expected to simply follow the diktats because the decisions are taken by those 'who know all' for the best of China. The Han Chinese hold the view that China is a gift for those 'unfortunate' enough to have been born outside of its heavenly-defined boundaries. From Confucius downwards, they have been puzzled as to why others cannot see and accept this simple and amiable reality.

However, underlying this simplicity are a number of historical perspectives, reasoning and experiences that the Chinese society has gone through. These range from their self-belief to geopolitical experiences.

Components of Chinese Characteristics

This paper lists the six components that makeup quite the characteristics of China, in no particular order, and explicates ontologically on each one's contribution to our overall inquest. These components are not only folklore in China but are also extensively included in textbooks in order to shape a national identity. Unlike its 'iron brother' Pakistan's 'identity crisis' because of the latter's obsession with being 'anything but Indian', the identity crisis of China is not due to lineage but due to the need to shape the narrative and exploit it for CCP's particular agenda.

- Heavenly Mandate
- The Concept of the Middle Kingdom
- Strategic Culture
- Single, Central Leadership
- Confucianism
- Lessons from the 'Century of Humiliation'

Heavenly Mandate

The idea of 'Heaven' is deeply embedded in the social mores of the Chinese since the time a group of people set up habitats on the shores and flood-plains of the raging Yellow River over two millennia ago. In all great civilisations, such widely held and well-accepted beliefs naturally seep into governance. For example, the idea of *'Vasudhaiva Khutumbakam'* (The world is one) is not only deeply ingrained in our ethos but is also a cornerstone of our international relationships and practice of statecraft. An understanding of how 'Heaven' plays a central role in Chinese culture is, therefore, important to appreciate Chinese decisions even as it grows stronger, throws the gauntlet of a challenge at others and aspires to occupy the sole pole position as spelt out in the 'Chinese Dream of national rejuvenation' explained by Xi Jinping. The triple concepts of the Chinese Emperor being the 'Son of the Cosmic Order (also known as Heaven)' (*tianzi*) to rule the 'Middle Kingdom' (*zhongguo*) and be responsible for everything under the Heaven (*tianxia*) used to determine the behaviour of the Chinese Emperor and his subjects. Even a Communist like Mao Ze Dong thought it fit to proclaim the founding of People's Republic of China from Tian-an-men or the 'Gate of Heavenly Peace' on October 1, 1949. The idea of a 'New World Institution' proposed by the noted modern Chinese philosopher Zhao Tingyang in c. 2005 and 2009[4,5] expands on *tianxia* and the Confucian concept of harmony, much like what Xi Jinping is attempting to do now. Surprisingly, the Cultural Revolution of Mao which wanted to throw away all old practices and ideas labelling them as 'counter-revolutionary', did not or could not do so to these triple concepts.

It is a Chinese belief that outsiders (also referred to as 'uncooked' or 'barbarians', *shengfan*) could be *Sinicized* (*Hanhua*) or cooked and tamed (*shufan*) by making them adopt Chinese culture and customs. China is also referred to by various names such as *shenzhou* ('Divine Land') or *tianchao* ('Celestial Empire'), all denoting in unmistakable terms that the Chinese are the most privileged because they are Divinely appointed to rule the world, a privilege not given to others.

This belief in 'Heavenly Mandate' to rule the world gives the ordinary Chinese self-confidence. Since the CCP has effectively appropriated the Heavenly Mandate from the extinct Imperial dynasties to itself, this also gives the CCP members the confidence that whatever decisions they take, even harsh and unpalatable ones, would be understood and obeyed by the people in the firm belief that these are taken under the Heavenly Mandate and would be for their eventual good. Essentially the Standing Committee of the Politburo represented by the General Secretary—and now, the Paramount Leader—is the 'Heavenly Mandated' Emperor of the People's Republic of China.

Middle Kingdom

The Emperor, Son of Heaven, ruled everything under Heaven as Heaven's representative leading to the concept of the Middle Kingdom —midway between Heaven and other geographical regions. For various reasons, the littoral states of East Asia from Japan and Korea to Melaka and even beyond sometimes deferred to China, at various times for various intervals, in the period between 618 CE to 1912 CE. These nations accepted Chinese oversight, culture and knowledge as universal truths in return for Confucian knowledge, education, trade, culture and protection. Thus, was born the tributary system of the Middle Kingdom and the idea of *Pax Sinica*. The Emperor sent his emissaries to far away tributes on a regular basis to ensure their continued submission. The Chinese cannot even imagine that others could oppose their noble, benign and genuine intentions to elevate the non-Hans from their barbarianism! It is this so-called *benign* but expansionist mindset that made Mao proclaim his desire for the annexation of Tibet's palm and its five fingers, Nepal, Bhutan, Sikkim, Ladakh and the then NEFA (now, Arunachal Pradesh) without any sensitivity towards those regions or countries or people.

The idea of the Middle Kingdom inherently makes the Chinese believe that they can grab territory from others or even the Global Commons and that thought makes them feel superior to the others. Thus, it was the 11-dash line arbitrarily drawn over the South China Sea that was self-bestowed by the Kuomintang government in 1947. In 1953, in order to mitigate the conflict with neighbouring Vietnam, the current nine-dash line emerged when Beijing eliminated two of the dashes in the Gulf of Tonkin, as a favour from an Emperor to his ex-vassal state. The claim by Xi Jinping in the 19th National Congress (October 2017), while listing his government's achievements, "Construction on islands and reefs in the South China Sea has seen steady progress", thus nonchalantly defying the Permanent Court of Arbitration's (PCA) of July 12, 2016 award under UNCLOS, echoes a similar attitude. Through its local laws promulgated in c. 2014, China mandated that no fishing activity could take place in SCS without its authorisation. It also specified periods during which fishing was not allowed in SCS and penalties for violation, thereby trying to establish a de-facto control regime over its claimed territory. Claims over Sinkiang fall in the same category. Thus, the arrogant rejection of the UNCLOS arbitration and the continuing and prolonged unsettlement of either the boundary dispute with India or the Conduct of Parties (CoP) with the ASEAN. A day after the PCA's Award, China's Assistant Foreign Minister Liu Zhenmin said," We do not recognise or implement the award. We hope it is only white paper and it will not be enforced. Just dump it into the garbage or put it on a shelf or put it in archives and let us come back to the track of negotiations. We have set up one [ADIZ] over the East China Sea (close to Japan) and whether we will set up another in the South China Sea will depend on the degree of the threat we are facing. If threatened enough, we will do so but it will depend on a host of factors".

The strength of such ancient and deep-rooted ideas can be gauged by the fact that a Taiwan (ROC) which is facing a permanent threat of invasion from Mainland China and is left with very few friendly nations which recognise it, however, echoes the same ideas on Tibet, Xinjiang, South and East China Seas, etc. as PRC. Article 26 of the Constitution of RoC specifically refers to Tibet and Mongolia as their parts. Taiwan continued to maintain a "Mongolia, Tibet Affairs Commission" (MTAC), originally formed during the Qing rule, until 2017 after disbanding which the same functions are performed by the "Mongolian and Tibetan Cultural Center". Taiwan's continued claims in the South and East China Seas betray the same geostrategic mentality of Imperial China. Indeed, the vague and imprecise eleven-dash line, the precursor to today's nine-dash line on which PRC claims almost 90 per cent of South China Sea, was published by the Kuomintang (KMT, also known as China National People's Party) in 1936 and later officially in February 1948. The 1993 'Policy Guidelines for the South China Sea' issued by the ROC says, "The South China Sea area within the historic water limit is the maritime area under the jurisdiction of the Republic of China, where the Republic of China possesses all rights and interests." Due to pressure from other nations, most notably the US, RoC 'suspended' the 1993 Policy Guideline in December 2005 but has not revoked it. After the PCA's Arbitral award, RoC's Ministry of External Affairs said, "The ROC government reiterates that the South China Sea Islands are part of the territory of the ROC and that it will take resolute action to safeguard the country's territory and relevant maritime rights". [6] Both the ruling Democratic Progressive Party (DPP) and the opposition Kuomintang Party (KMT) opposed the Award. Since PRC's claims to the SCS under the nine-dash line rubric follow from a claim made during RoC's rule of Mainland China, its renunciation of claims now is likely to have an impact on PRC's stance as well at least legally, but RoC has so far not chosen to unequivocally do so, though there is a nuanced change in RoC's stance since May 2009 with it placing emphasis on islands and 'surrounding waters' rather than the whole 'water body' of South China Sea. Thus, it claims the four 'Sha group of islands and features' and their 'surrounding waters' as its own, that is Dongsha (Pratas), the Xisha (Paracels), the Zhongsha (Macclesfield Bank), and the Nansha (Spratlys). While other claimant states in SCS, namely Vietnam, Philippines, Malaysia and Brunei, make their claims from their coastal baselines, both PRC and RoC claim ownership of the four Sha islands, low-tide elevations and rocks and then define their positions outwards from these features, a position struck down by the PCA.

Strategic Culture

There is a strongly embedded 'strategic culture' in China, that is its culture influencing its strategy and goals. The strategic culture of a country is the result of the mutual influence of the political and cultural history of a country over a fairly long period of time.[2] Thus, it gives a country's population the ability to assess themselves as regards their strengths, weaknesses, opportunities, and threats based on their political and cultural continuum. In short, the 'strategic culture' of a country gives its people a sense of 'where they stand' in relation to other nation-states based on their 'past and the present' and how they should reach in the 'future' their pre-ordained 'strategic goals' that they so richly deserve. In the case of China, the set of strategic goals is shaped by such concepts as '*tianxia*' (All Under Heaven), '*zhongguo*' (Middle Kingdom) and "*t'ien-ming*" (Mandate of the Heaven). In countries with long civilisations, 'culture' is a core concept because, as Huntington calls them, they are 'civilizational identities'.[3] These 'civilizational identities' are not easily mutable unlike ideologies, rules of law, international relationships, etc. This sense was what prompted the State Councilor and the then Foreign Minister, Yang Jiechi to make the statement in the 17th ASEAN Regional Forum (ARF, August 2017), "China is a big country and you are small countries, and that is just a fact". That not only meant comparison of geographical sizes, but more importantly implied tributes paid by most of these countries to China at various times in history. In other words, he was referring to the emerging New World Order (NWO) with China at the apex in the backdrop of Chinese history and the message was intended to go far and wide beyond the ASEAN.

This theory of Samuel Huntington can be juxtaposed with those of two other near contemporaries of his, Francis Fukuyama of the US and Paul Kennedy of Britain. While Fukuyama argued that the ideological war among nations was over and 'liberal democracies' have taken over, which seemed quite right by the 1990s until possibly mid-2010s, Paul Kennedy argued that the fall of Great Powers was ordained by their over-reach without a concomitant resource-base to support their ambitions. Fukuyama's theory was all right until subverted by an authoritarian cabal (neither 'liberal nor 'democratic') of China which has inched the region ever so closer to war since the outbreak of the COVID pandemic. Paul Kennedy's theory may be about to come true in the case of China where the resource-base it lacks is 'friendly nations'.

The 'strategic culture' of a country defines the universal set of its strategic narrative while the 'strategic posture' is a time-varying manifestation of this strategic culture based on the current capabilities, geopolitical situations and aspirations of the country. It is a point-in-time reality or abstraction of the 'strategic culture'. The strategic posture is what the external world sees or experiences from a particular country. The strategic posture could even vary with a change in political leadership, relative global power, inventory of weapons and such. The prosecution of the strategic posture is not always to achieve the strategic goal(s) as dictated by the strategic culture. That can be achieved only through a series of steps and the extant 'posture' is only a steppingstone. If 'strategic culture' is ideational, then 'strategic posture' is the physical tool to achieve parts of the strategic goals.

The strategic culture requires a state to employ all the resources of the state to achieve a particular strategic posture. As the resources of the state wax and wane, so does the strategic posture. As advances are made in science, technology, economy, politics, international relationship, etc., corresponding adjustments are made to the strategic posture and as reverses are encountered, the instantaneous strategic posture is scaled down too. But the strategic culture remains intact, unaffected by these fluctuations. As China has made significant advances in various fields in the last decade, such as Artificial Intelligence, Computing, Networking, Diplomacy, etc., its 'strategic posture' has also changed. Missiles like DF-21 carrier killers, the hypersonic glide DF-17, MIRVd DF-41 ICBMs, ASAT (Anti-SATellite) weapons, killer drone swarms, H-6 strategic bombers, Type 094/096 SSBNs with their load of JL-2/JL-3 SLBMs have convinced China that it can up the *ante* as far as strategic posture goes. If one is not careful with orchestration, the process of escalation can easily lead to war as it almost happened at Galwan, even if one did not intend it.

The September 2011 white paper[7] released by the Information Office of the State Council entitled *China's Peaceful Development* listed its core interests as—(1) state sovereignty; (2) national security; (3) territorial integrity and national reunification; (4) China's political system established by the Constitution and overall social stability; (5) basic safeguards for ensuring sustainable economic and social development. This is an example of the 'strategic posture' of China as of that time. Of course, the real intentions are couched in pious statements such as China "... never engages in aggression or expansion, never seeks hegemony, and remains a staunch force for upholding regional and world peace and stability" and ". . . China does not seek regional hegemony or sphere of influence", found in that White Paper. But China's actions since PRC was founded have been quite the opposite. Amidst its on-going land aggression in Ladakh and maritime aggression in SCS and the East China Sea and COVID-engendered 'Wolf Warrior' diplomacy, Xi Jinping spoke of "vision of a community with a shared future . . . open and inclusive development . . . [China working as a] builder of global peace, a contributor to global development and a defender of international order" in the 75th Session of the UN on September 22, 2020.

Therefore, strategic posture is, oxymoronically, tactical in nature and could confuse or mislead another nation if the foundational and time-invariant 'strategic culture' is not understood. For example, while the various Imperial dynasties expanded the borders of China, some more and others less, the capture of the Ming Emperor (the great-grandson of the redoubtable Yongle Emperor) by the Mongols in c. 1449 shut the doors on future wars by a Han Chinese Emperor until the Manchus (non-Hans), especially Emperor Qianlong, reversed that decision. Similarly, Mao Ze Dong, fresh from his victorious Long March and the founding of the People's Republic of China decided power projection was the best choice and took part in the Korean War immediately and later started wars with both India and the USSR. Similarly, though Deng Xiao Ping ordered an attack on Vietnam to 'teach them a lesson' in c. 1979, he later adopted a *24-Character Strategy* that led to a temporary pause in the larger pursuit of 'strategic goals' but was actually meant to further strengthen the power to achieve the goals of the 'strategic culture' silently. His successors Jiang Zemin and Hu Jintao largely abided by that strategy until Xi Jinping decided that the long-term and discreet 'strategic posture' needed to be revised, especially after the outbreak of the Pandemic in c. 2020.

The Strategic posture should ideally embrace every aspect of the State in order to maximise the benefits and successfully achieve the ideas of the strategic culture. What would the achievement of such a strategic posture bring to the people of the land? That is the dream that needs to be 'sold' to the people in order to enlist their wholehearted support for the prosecution of the strategic culture, a path that may be quite painful too to the people and the State at times. In Xi Jinping's idea of the 'Chinese Dream', the economic well-being of the State and its subjects are intertwined with the worldwide ascendancy of the Chinese military and power. For example, the ban on import of coal from Australia after the Australian Government called for probing the origins of the Wuhan Corona Virus, led to power rationing in many parts of China, silently borne by the citizens in the best interests of the nations. The Chinese rulers always knew, including the Communist successors of the Imperial Dynasties, that they would rule only until they provided prosperity, peace and stability. The 'Dream' and 'Rejuvenation' are therefore quite understandable terminologies.

The Chinese Dream is therefore a euphemism for the Chinese Strategic Culture and its Goals. The strategic culture and goals of China always reflect in the Constitution of the CCP. The idea of the CCP is to tell the Chinese that strategic goals can be achieved only by the CCP. Jiang Zemin, who unexpectedly became the President in c. 1993 introduced his idea of 'Three Represents' into the CCP Constitution. The Three Represents were in Jiang Zemin's words ". . . it [CCP] has always represented the development trend of China's advanced productive forces, the orientation of China's advanced culture, and the fundamental interests of the overwhelming majority of the Chinese people". While the term 'advanced productive forces' referred to capitalists, 'fundamental interests of the overwhelming majority of the Chinese people' is the 'great rejuvenation of the Chinese people' (or, more popularly, 'Chinese Dream') expounded by Xi Jinping on November 29, 2012, as the new General Secretary of the CCP. However, this has also been expounded by others in different terms, for example, Deng Xiaoping called it 'invigoration of China' even as he broke away from the traditional Marxist-Leninist theory, and Jiang Zemin, 'great rejuvenation of the Chinese nation'. Xi Jinping has cleverly intertwined nationalism with rejuvenation by suggesting, 'rejuvenation after a hundred years of humiliation'. So is the case with

Xi Jinping's 'Thought on Socialism with *Chinese Characteristics* for a New Era'. The thirteenth pillar of the fourteen pillars on which Xi Jinping based his *Thoughts* is "Promoting the Building of a Community with a Shared Future for Mankind". In his speech to the 19th Congress (October 2017), he mentioned the 'Belt and Road Initiative' (BRI) eight times and meshed them with his call for "discussion and collaboration" for "shared interest" and "shared growth" with other countries. By thus smartly linking BRI with CPC's Constitution, the 'economic project' has undergone a thorough strategic transformation. The BRI is now a strategic goal, as much as Taiwan and the South China Sea are. This is how the strategic culture of China manifests.

The 'Chinese Characteristics' are a constant reminder to the Chinese people that every action of the State, every legislation that is passed, every decision that is taken, every innovation that is done is laced with appropriate aspects of the strategic culture. The Chinese Characteristics are the basic building blocks that help the State achieve a strategic posture which in turn assure concomitant prosperity for the people.

Single Central Leadership

The Chinese are used to a single central leadership in the form of dynastic emperors without a break for over 3,000 years. Therefore, the autocratic leadership of either Mao Ze Dong or Xi Jinping did not cause a ripple. Even the devastating decisions of the Great Leap Forward or Cultural Revolution were largely accepted. When Mao Ze Dong decided to establish, suddenly, a diplomatic relationship with the 'bourgeoise Americans' after having denounced them all through his life, the decision was simply accepted by the people. There was some opposition from the likes of Gen. Lin Biao which was appropriately taken care of. Similarly, when Deng Xiaoping decided later to open the economy and collaborate with the US, there was no opposition either. So also, the current aggression and the 'Wolf Warrior' diplomacy by Xi Jinping.

While Chairman Mao was embroiled in Communism and constant revolution, Xi Jinping is more concerned with 'order and stability' to achieve the Chinese Dream. These are the two main thoughts that all Sons of Heaven of all Dynasties had constantly striven to achieve. His disappearance for a few weeks before his election in the 17th CCP Congress in November 2012 was because he demanded that he be given the top three posts of General Secretary of the CCP, President of PRC and the Chairman of the Central Military Commission (CMC) all at once. In his calculations, anything short would not let him achieve 'order and stability'. Of course, during the course of his first term, he added other powerful positions to his portfolio and became an Absolute Emperor in the process.

One recent example of how this single central leadership works in a China that is accustomed to this sort of governance for over 3000 years is when drought in May followed by heavy rains in July 2020 caused a 'double jeopardy' in the food security situation in China. Though the food stocks are comfortable, President Xi Jinping emphasized grain security by not wasting food, in two speeches, one in Jilin in July and the other in early August. It soon became a national rage and a campaign started automatically with restaurants starting to serve smaller portions, TV channels and websites banning food shows, etc. all done without a prompt or a legislation! Another example is the decision not to announce the casualty figures of PLA in the recent Galwan incident, a decision which was implicitly accepted by the Chinese at large. A typical mindset of centralisation also manifests, for example, in the new Chinese proposal to alter the basic architecture of the Internet Protocol (IP) to make it centralised[8] while the whole architecture has moved towards distributed processing and control for decades.

Xi and his comrades in CCP have internalized two things very well. One, the main cause for the disappearance of a very powerful Soviet Union by the end of 1991 was liberalisation such as Demokratizatsiya, Glasnost and Perestroika. The other is the thesis by Alfred Thayer

Mahan, the American Naval and Strategic Expert, about the central importance of the Navy in power projection. For a CCP-dominated China, whose real aim is *tianxia* under *t'ien-ming*, the second point is very important but that cannot be achieved unless and until the lesson learnt from USSR is firstly absorbed. Therefore, one of the major goals of Xi has been to tighten the control of CCP in every sphere of activity within China. Xi said in 2013 that the reformist policies adopted by Deng cannot negate the 30 years of achievements that came before. It is worth remembering that in c. 1981, Deng Xiao Ping had said that the Cultural Revolution by Mao was a "gross error".

Confucianism

Confucianism plays a major part not only in the internal governance of China but also in its international relationship. The five important concepts of Confucianism, equality, harmony, decency, virtue and pacifism directly map into what China claims as its core foreign policy, the *Panchsheel*. Two Confucian concepts are important for understanding some of China's latest actions: Everything has its place and there must be harmony.

An important tenet of Confucius has been 'Know Thy Place' though some might interpret it differently. But there is no ambiguity about the 'hierarchy' that was fundamental in the thoughts of Confucius. Thus, 'hierarchy' played a stellar role not only in internal governance but also in external governance. The Chinese Emperors never failed to make their neighbours know 'Their Places' expecting them to prostrate in front of them with their foreheads touching the ground, and even more so whenever they transgressed. The 'Son of Heaven' has the mandate to restore the 'natural order of the Universe' as determined by the Chinese Emperor. The reason that China has attributed for the on-going skirmish and stand-off in Ladakh is that 'India transgressed' by building infrastructure in forward areas. 'Everything has its place' immediately puts China at the apex and everyone else subservient. It is said that Confucius even lived among the *barbarians*, that is non-Hans, because he believed that Sinicization would make them *civil*. That was precisely the reason[9,10] that Mao Ze Dong decided to attack India at an opportune time in 1962 when the attention of both the USA and USSR were on the Cuban Missile Crisis. The 'Everything has its place' was also the reason that in 1979 when Deng Xiao Ping ordered an attack on Vietnam to 'put it in its place', even as our then External Affairs Minister Vajpayee was in Beijing.

Hu Jintao proposed 'harmonious ocean' concept for economic globalisation and regional economic integration. There is no wonder that he is credited as the architect of modern PLAN, making it a 'strategic force' by c. 2008.[11] The 'harmonious ocean' concept implies acceptance of Chinese claims of the nine-dash line in the South China Sea (beginning 2013, China is surreptitiously introducing another dash making it a ten-dash line) and its other claims in the East China Sea.

However, there were two periods when there was an intense rejection of Confucius, one in the distant past of the brief Qin-dynasty rule and the other after the collapse of the Qing dynasty in 1911, more particularly during Mao's rule, when even the graves of Confucius and his descendants were vandalised as part of Cultural Revolution.[12] However, Xi is restoring Confucius to his usual high pedestal in China now.

The Chinese Foreign Minister Wang Yi's first statement upon assuming office was ". . . efforts to build a harmonious world of sustained peace and common prosperity". Wang Yi suggested, after the Doka La incident, "Both the countries should seek harmonious relations ... " In a US-China Business Council meet, Wang Yi elaborated, "Over 2,000 years ago, Chinese sage Confucius observed that 'A gentleman seeks harmony without uniformity whereas a petty man does just the opposite'. "In his post-COVID European tour to ease the tension with the US, Wang Yi was again "seeking harmony without uniformity". Speaking in European Policy Center in 2019, Wang Yi said, "Confucius said something similar 2,500 years ago, 'All living things should grow in harmony without hurting one another; and all the ways should move forward without interfering with one another', the implication being that other nations should not interfere with China as it moves naturally towards assuming its apex position in the NWO.

Lessons from the 'Century of Humiliation'

As Hong Kong dived deep into months of protests, we go back to look at the most iconic protests of them all, the Students Uprising at the Tiananmen Square way back in the period between April and June 1989, an event also referred to as 1989 Democracy Movement. While Hong Kongers have a different approach to democracy, the youth of Mainland China today are patriotic and supportive of the Establishment, which means the CCP and its authority. The difference between today's youth of Mainland China and those of 1989 is predicated upon 'historical memory' that has been forcibly fed to them by the CCP as a lesson learnt from the 1989 incidents.[13] Four words, *wuwang guochi* ('Never forget national humiliation') are commonly found everywhere. Of course, such 'historical memories' that lead to a 'national identity' are invariably political in nature and can be controversial in a large, diverse, pluralistic democratic country such as India but in a centralised, homogenised country such as China under the CCP, it is easier to mould a particular narrative, like a shaped charge. The PLA helped Mao Zedong popularise his ideas through the 'Little Red Book' and the same PLA is now devising strategies to spread Xi's Thoughts likewise.

The Chinese remember the period between the mid-1800 to mid-1900 as a painful period of humiliation when China was bullied by imperialism of various flavours of various countries. In China, efforts have been made to embed the humiliation deep into Chinese minds. This 'collective memory' permeates all aspects of Chinese governance, especially its foreign policy. This is the biggest differentiator between the democracy-inspired people of Hong Kong and the Humiliation-inspired people of Mainland China, for example, today. The period between 1839 and 1949 is considered by the CCP as the Century of Humiliation, starting with the defeat of the Manchu Emperor in the First Opium War in 1839, followed by opening five entrepots for British trade, the Treaty of the Bogue which most unpalatably made the Emperor recognise Britain as its equal and forced him to grant exemptions to Britishers from Chinese laws and prosecution, coming especially after the Qing Commissioner on Opium Trade, Lin Zexu, wrote a letter on January 15, 1840, to Queen

Victoria, "The barbarian merchants of your country, if they wish to do business for a long period, are required to obey our statutes respectfully and to cut off permanently the source of opium. They must, by no means, try to test the effectiveness of the law with their lives". Such a Bogue-like concession was later demanded by and conceded to American and French subjects too later. The ceding of Hong Kong to Britain, and the destruction of the summer palace in Beijing (*Yuanmingyuan*) during the Second Opium War also added to more humiliation. The French and the Americans also joined the British with the American gunboats traversing the Chinese rivers at will for nearly a hundred years. The Japanese attacked China in 1894 and took over Manchuria, Taiwan and the vassal state of Korea. The Boxer Revolution was put down by an alliance of eight nations and when the Manchu Dynasty collapsed in 1912, the Japanese occupied even more parts of China and demanded compliance with its 21-point ultimatum in c. 1915. In c. 1931, Japan occupied Manchuria and by c. 1937 large sections of China came under the control of the Japanese Emperor. In c. 1940, the Chinese forces of Kuomintang and the CCP were on the brink of a total rout. It was the American help through India that largely helped the Chinese forces until Japan surrendered to the Allies and quit China in c. 1945.

While these are historic facts and traumatic for any country, it was the skilful constant harking back to the 'Century of Humiliation' that provided legitimacy to Mao Ze Dong's government despite his blunders of 'Great Leap Forward' and 'Cultural Revolution' which only led to famine, anarchy and death of millions of Chinese. Contrast these Chinese humiliations with those suffered by India for several centuries and modern-day India's veritable acceptance of the history within the right context and frame. While the 'Humiliation' has been referred to incessantly by all top Communist leaders, Xi Jinping has vividly morphed that into 'rejuvenation', thus linking economic and military might as the twin pillars of his idea of 'Chinese Dream' emanating from 'Humiliation'. In order to sustain these efforts, a massive attempt at social engineering[14] starting from uniform school textbooks has been launched by the Xi

Jinping regime. Xi Jinping's thoughts are being taught in prestigious Tsinghua & Renmin Universities.

The top Chinese leaders have carefully studied war history, especially the history of Europe as the US Naval strategist Alfred Thayer Mahan did, and are convinced that sea power is essential for conquering the world and re-imagining the more-spanning Middle Kingdom than what, for example, the Yongle Emperor of the Ming Dynasty did with his Admiral Zheng He. The Chinese PLAN policymakers and the top politicians of the Standing Committee and the Politburo have also internalised Thayer Mahan's doctrine that naval power is essential to achieving great power status. His monumental work is a compulsory read within PLAN. Many Chinese analysts believe that the de-emphasis of naval power for four centuries, after Yongle's period, proved disastrous for China and the 'Century of Humiliation' happened because of that when gunboats moving with impunity up and down the coasts as well as the Yangtze established foreign dominance.

For a country which has maintained historical records of nearly 2500 years, the Century of Humiliation is too recent and too traumatic to be forgotten, something that has come in handy for CCP to inflame passions and attempt to achieve strategic goals.

Conclusion

The attempt here has been to 'deconstruct' the 'Chinese Characteristics' in terms of dominant ideational precepts practised by Chinese society and its Dynasties. Such a deconstruction is needed in getting to the root of the Chinese behaviour in recent months after COVID struck China and spread everywhere. The Chinese behaviour whether it is in the East or South China Seas and Ladakh has been militarily aggressive especially along the Line of Actual Control (LAC) with India. The Chinese behaviour with Australia and several European countries have been to be 'diplomatically and economically aggressive' earning them the sobriquet, 'The Wolf Warriors'. In the opinion of many, Cold War 2.0 is already upon us with China being the second pole unlike the USSR in the last version, though its characteristics are different. As increasingly the right-thinking world unites against such behaviour, through Quad or Quad-plus or other formal and informal groupings, it becomes imperative to look deep into Chinese history through openings in the bamboo curtain so as to predict their aspirations and likely future actions and take effective measures to contain any adverse fallout. The basic building blocks of the 'Chinese Characteristics' clearly suggest that the Chinese objective is to be an unrivalled and sole hegemon as per the timelines of President Xi Jinping.

Notes

1. "United States Strategic Approach to the People's Republic of China", May 20, 2020 https://www.whitehouse.gov/wp-content/uploads/2020/05/U.S.-Strategic-Approach-to-The-Peoples-Republic-of-China-Report-5.20.20.pdf, accessed on October 23, 2020.

2. "Strategic Culture and Pragmatic National Interest", Nayef Al-Rodhan, Global Policy, Jul. 22, 2015, https://www.globalpolicyjournal.com/blog/22/07/2015/strategic-culture-and-pragmatic-national-interest, accessed on October 23, 2020.

3. "The Clash of Civilizations and the Remaking of World Order", Samuel P.Huntington, Simon & Schuster, 1996, accessed on October 23, 2020.

4. "The Tianxia System: An Introduction to the Philosophy of a World nstitution", Zhao Tingyang, 2005, http://www.chinaheritagequarterly.org/tien-hsiaphp?searchterm=021_utopia.inc&issue=021, , accessed on October 23, 2020.

5. "Investigations of the Bad World: Political Philosophy as the First Philosophy", Zhao Tingyang, 2009, http://www.chinaheritagequarterly.org/tien-hsia.php?searchterm=021_utopia.inc&issue=021, accessed on October 23, 2020.

6. "Taiwan: South China Sea Ruling Completely Unacceptable", Shannon Tiezi, The Diplomat, Jul. 13, 2016, https://thediplomat.com/2016/07/taiwan-south-china-sea-ruling-completely-unacceptable/,, accessed on October 23, 2020.

7. "China's Peaceful Development", Information Office of the State Council, Sep. 2011, http://english.www.gov.cn/archive/white_paper/2014/09/09/content_281474986284646.htm, , accessed on October 23, 2020.

8. "New Internet Protocol: Redesigning the Internet with Chinese Characteristics?", Munish Sharma, Manohar Parrikar- IDSA, October 15, 2020 https://idsa.in/idsacomments/new-internet-protocol-msharma-151020, , accessed on October 23, 2020.

9.   "Who Started the Fighting?", R.S.Kalha, Manohar Parrikar-IDSA, Oct. 17, 2012 https://idsa.in/idsacomments/Whostartedthefighting%3F_R.S.Kalha_171012

10. "The 1962 Lessons", Prakash Nanda, Indian Defence Review, Oct. 20, 2014 http://www.indiandefencereview.com/news/the-1962-lessons/, , accessed on October 23, 2020.

11. "The History of the Twenty-First-Century Chinese Navy", Bernard D Cole, Naval War College Review, Vol. 67, No 3, https://digital-commons.usnwc.edu/cgi/viewcontent.cgi?article=1292&context=nwc-review, , accessed on October 23, 2020.

12. "China's Enthusiastic Re-Embrace of Confucius", Gabrielle Jaffe, The Atlantic, Oct. 7, 2013, https://www.theatlantic.com/china/archive/2013/10/chinas-enthusiastic-re-embrace-of-confucius/280326/, accessed on October 23, 2020.

13. "History, identity, and security: Producing and consuming nationalism in China", William A Callahan Critical Asian Studies, 38:2, 179-208, https://doi.org/10.1080/14672710600671087, accessed on October 23, 2020.

14. "The Past's Transformative Power", Zheng Wang, The Wilson Quarterly, Fall 2020, https://www.wilsonquarterly.com/quarterly/the-ends-of-history/the-pasts-transformative-power/?emci=2e6f636f-290e-eb11-96f5-00155d03affc&emdi=5f6024ca-0c13-eb11-96f5-00155d03affc&ceid=46413, accessed on October 23, 2020.

Reading the Tea Leaves: Chinese Strategic Thought

Balasubramanian C

The term "Geopolitics" in the modern sense is a western concept. The history of the term 'geo-politics' can date back to 1899 when the term was first coined by the Swedish political scientist Rudolf Kjellen. Its use spread throughout Europe in the period between World Wars I and II (1918–39) and came into worldwide use during the latter.

An Eastern Civilization like China has a distinctive way of conceiving how geography shapes their existence in the world in relation to other entities. In its millennial history, China has developed a distinct geopolitical outlook that influences its foreign policy still today.

Chinese Strategic Thought

The chief principle to examine to understand China's geopolitical perception is to examine the philosophical pillars upon which it is based. There are three hierarchical levels:

- The Family
- The Kingdom
- The World

They should be organised in a hierarchical but harmonious way where each element has its role and pursues it for stability of the system.

In practice, keeping order in the kingdom means ensuring peace at home by preserving the sovereignty of the state, while maintaining the world order rendered into establishing an international system that grants China's security.

Confucianism

With a focus on Peace and Harmony, Confucianism disallowed expansionism and considered war as a last resort that was to be waged only for defensive purposes. But in practice, this was always not the case, throughout history, China has recurrently sought to expand its borders to increase its power, control vital trade routes along the Silk Route and improve its own security. These aspects are closely related to the traditional concept of Tianxia (天下), which means "All under the Heaven", a concise way of speaking of the traditional Chinese vision of the world order.

In ancient China, the emperor was a guarantor of peace and harmony which had to be ensured on a universal scale covering everything located under the heaven. However, this was never achieved, as rival states, tribes and kingdoms outside of China's sovereignty have always existed. This resulted in the Chinese developing a "concentric view" of the international system. At the core laid China (Zhōngguó- 中国) itself, considered to the centre of the world in geographical and cultural terms. Chinese civilization was considered superior to that of adjacent populations deemed as non-civilized and barbarians. It also perceived China as a "beacon of culture" that can shape over to neighbouring and rival kingdoms, people and civilised them.

Ying Yang Juxtaposition

Courtesy: Wikipedia Commons

A second significant feature is the "Ying Yang" (陰陽/阴阳) juxtaposition described by Taoism. The Ying is regarded as feminine, moon and subordinate element, while the Yang is the masculine, sun, creative and dominant one. The two coexist and blend in a harmonious manner. In times of war, this is interpreted as initially adopting a passive stance and then performing a counter-attack from a position of strength. Such belief is reflected in the writings of Sun Tzu in his book "The Art of War". Sun Tzu mentions the Tao, which means the way, and describes ways to dynamically combine stillness and movement to defeat the enemy. Sun Tzu insists on military leaders to avoid a direct confrontation, especially when the bulk of enemy forces, and instead control in the areas where the adversary is weak by exploiting the potential of the situation. This is to be done by waiting or by vigorously creating an opportunity allowing to strike from a position of strength, either by deceiving or outmanoeuvring the adversary. The ultimate aim and supreme achievement of the general are to win a war without fighting, so as to triumph in a cost-effective manner.

These concepts are deeply ingrained in Chinese strategic thinking, as they are found in other works such as those of Sun Bin in his treatise also named "The Art of War", a supposed descendant of Sun Tzu and the lesser-known treatise "Hundred Unorthodox Strategies" whose author remains unknown and controversial.

Game of GO: Chinese Strategic Play

Courtesy: Wikipedia Commons

Thirdly is the game of "GO" (Weiqi 围棋), an ancient Chinese strategy board game played to the present day. The exact origin of Go is unknown, but the game has long been regarded as an exercise in discipline and strategic thinking. This strategy board game resembles chess, although the two games differ profoundly. There are two players, one using white stones and the other black ones. On each turn, the player must place a stone on the board, which is initially empty. Depending on how it places the stones, the player can turn the opponents' one into its own. But in actuality, GO is actually way more complex than chess it requires much skill and most of all, a comprehensive long term vision, as it all depends on appropriately placing the stones in a strategic manner to control the largest area of the board. Fundamentally the game is about creating a sphere of influence greater than the other player. As it can be seen today, China is applying the principles of GO to extend its global influence.

Self-Conception

Like all great civilizations, China considers itself to be the centre of the world. In Chinese, it reflects this conception as Zhōngguó (中国), which means the Middle Kingdom. Through much of its history, China's borders were much smaller than the present ones. Its territory was limited to the large coastal strip of agricultural plains fortified by the Yellow River and the Yangtze River Basins. This region was the Economic, Demographic and Cultural Hub of the realm where the Han population concentrated. The concern was dealing with the other people. Throughout history, the Chinese rulers have attempted to solve the issue by integrating other kingdoms into a "Sino Centric Vassal" System. Subject states had to recognise Chinese 'suzerainty' and offer some tribute. But the whole issue was often largely symbolic and the vassal states were in essence autonomous.

Yet this allowed china to maintain positive relations and ensure the safety of its borders. Despite which the Chinese under the Ming Dynasty occasionally launched military campaigns to protect their vassals as in the case of the Korean Joseon Kingdom against the Japanese invasion in the late 16th Century. They also attacked neighbouring territories like Vietnam, which was invaded multiple times under Ming and Qing dynasties of China.

The matter was more problematic for the Chinese in the case of nomadic tribes in the north. They represented a constant threat for China for centuries and on two occasions they managed to conquer the country and establish imperial dynasties as in the case of the Mongol Yuan Dynasty in the 13th Century and the Manchu Qing Dynasty in the 17th Century.

Against these barbarians' tribes, the Chinese resorted to numerous strategies to keep the nomads out, including engineering, warfare, and diplomacy. Upon lack of choice but to set up defensive positions along the border, the Great Wall was constructed and military campaigns were conducted to eliminate the threat.

In the occurrence of a foreign tribe managing to conquer China then the Chinese relied on Soft Power. They were self-assured that their culture would absorb the invaders and turn them into Chinese. And this was proved in the case of the Yuan and the Qing Dynasties which eventually became one with Chinese characteristics. Despite its imperfections, the "China Centric System" continued to exist for centuries until the might of the western powers and Japan drew China into submission. This tragic period lasted from 1839–1949 which China regards as the "Century of Humiliation", which is a crucial component of the national identity of modern China. Since its formation, The PRC has implemented a strategy to preserve its sovereignty and territorial integrity including preventing foreign interferences and this is largely based upon thesecentury-old principles.

China Today

China wants to protect its core which still consists of the coastal area along the two great rivers the Yellow River (Huang He) and the Yangtze. This hydro-basin hosts the vast majority of the Han Population and is the country's economic heart where the main cities lie including its industrial and financial centres.

China perceives threats against this region from the sea or from the land. The need to defend the coastline from foreign aggression is one of the reasons why China has been building up its Navy and has built its "Anti-Access and Area Denial" (A2/AD) Platforms like long-range anti-ship ballistic missiles. China's primary concern is to deter or defeat a US intervention, most notably in the case of a contingency over Taiwan. In this logic, it developed a strategy based on three defence layers to keep the US forces far from its coasts.

On the land side, the threat of nomad tribes has disappeared, but to protect its heartland China still wants to control a vast buffer zone to increase its strategic depth which partially explains China's actions under Mao Zedong in his 'Right Palm Five Fingers' strategy. Mao described Tibet as right palm and Ladakh, Sikkim, Bhutan, Nepal and Arunachal Pradesh its five fingers. The regions of Xinxiang and Tibet were swiftly occupied immediately after the creation of China and also the intention behind the current leadership President Xi Jinping is determined to keep these two regions under control.

In this sense it can be explained to see China as an island, the western areas are a buffer zone to protect China's core, just like the sea is to the east. In the territorial disputes China is involved in the South China Sea, it is implementing the classic principles of Chinese strategy.

It seeks to avoid an open confrontation and, in many cases, (employing Classic Strategy of 'Art of winning without a fight') it employs paramilitary forces and naval militias to assert its claim in the South China Sea without resorting to the military and it gradually builds facilities and deploys its forces to strengthen its position.

Finally, amid a revival of Confucianism at the state level, the old conception of a "Harmonious Sino Centric Order" has reemerged under President Xi Jinping. China is representing it's One Belt One Road (OBOR) Initiative including its Maritime Silk Route (MSR) as a peaceful and mutually beneficially project, but it still reveals the one that has China at the centre.

In addition, many geopolitical observers note that the strategy China is employing in building these infrastructures resembles the game of GO, by gradually positioning these facilities and then by linking them together China is slowly expanding its sphere of influence not only across Eurasia and the Indo—Pacific but also Africa and South America. This portrays that China not only has its distinctive geopolitical conception but that it has a deep influence in China and understanding it is important to assess and counter the Chinese current strategy.

References

"Geopolitics." Encyclopædia Britannica. Encyclopædia Britannica, inc., n.d. https://www.britannica.com/topic/geopolitics.

"Tianxia天下." The China Story, April 7, 2020. https://www.thechinastory. org/yearbooks/yearbook-2013/forum-politics-and-society/tianxia-%E5%A4%A9%E4%B8%8B/.

"Ralph Sawyer." Ralph Sawyer—One Hundred Unorthodox Strategies: Battle and Tactics of Chinese Warfare. Accessed on October 15, 2021. https://www. ralphsawyer.com/one_hundred_unorthodox_strategies__battle_and_tactics_ of_chinese_warfare_23626.htm.

"The Game of Go: Ancient Applications and Contemporary Connotations 围棋游戏：古代应用及当代内涵." US, June 7, 2016. https://china.usc.edu/game-go-ancient-applications-and-contemporary-connotations-%E5%9B%B4%E6%A3%8B%E6%B8%B8%E6%88%8F%EF%BC%9A%E5%8F%A4%E4%BB%A3%E5%BA%94%E7%94%A8%E5%8F%8A%E5%BD%93%E4%BB%A3%E5%86%85%E6%B6%B5.

"History of Japan–Korea Relations." Wikipedia. Wikimedia Foundation, October 8, 2021. https://en.wikipedia.org/wiki/History_of_Japan%E2%80%93Korea_relations#Early_modern_period_(16th_%E2%80%93_18th_centuries).

"China–Vietnam Relations." Wikipedia. Wikimedia Foundation, October 12, 2021. https://en.wikipedia.org/wiki/China%E2%80%93Vietnam_relations#Early_history.

"Did the Great Wall of China Work?" History. National Geographic, May 3, 2021. https://www.nationalgeographic.com/history/history-magazine/article/the-great-wall-of-china.

"China's Anti-Access Area Denial." Missile Defense Advocacy Alliance. Accessed on October 15, 2021. https://missiledefenseadvocacy.org/missile-threat-and-proliferation/todays-missile-threat/china/china-anti-access-area-denial/.

Editor, "Mao Described Tibet Right Palm and Ladakh, Sikkim, Bhutan, Nepal and Arunachal Five Fingers." *Tibetan Journal*, November 3, 2017. http://www.tibetanjournal.com/mao-described-tibet-right-palm-ladakh-sikkim-bhutan-nepal-arunachal-five-fingers/.

www.ingramcontent.com/pod-product-compliance
Lightning Source LLC
Chambersburg PA
CBHW060508160726
47992CB00003B/1381